WINGSPREAD

The history of a place where ideas that make a difference are born and nurtured and grow.

Written by CRAIG CANINE

THE JOHNSON FOUNDATION, INC.
Racine, Wisconsin

© 1997 by The Johnson Foundation, Inc.
All rights reserved.
Printed in the United States of America
97 00 00   5 4 3 2 1

Library of Congress Catalog Card Number: 97-90639

ISBN 0-9641794-1-5

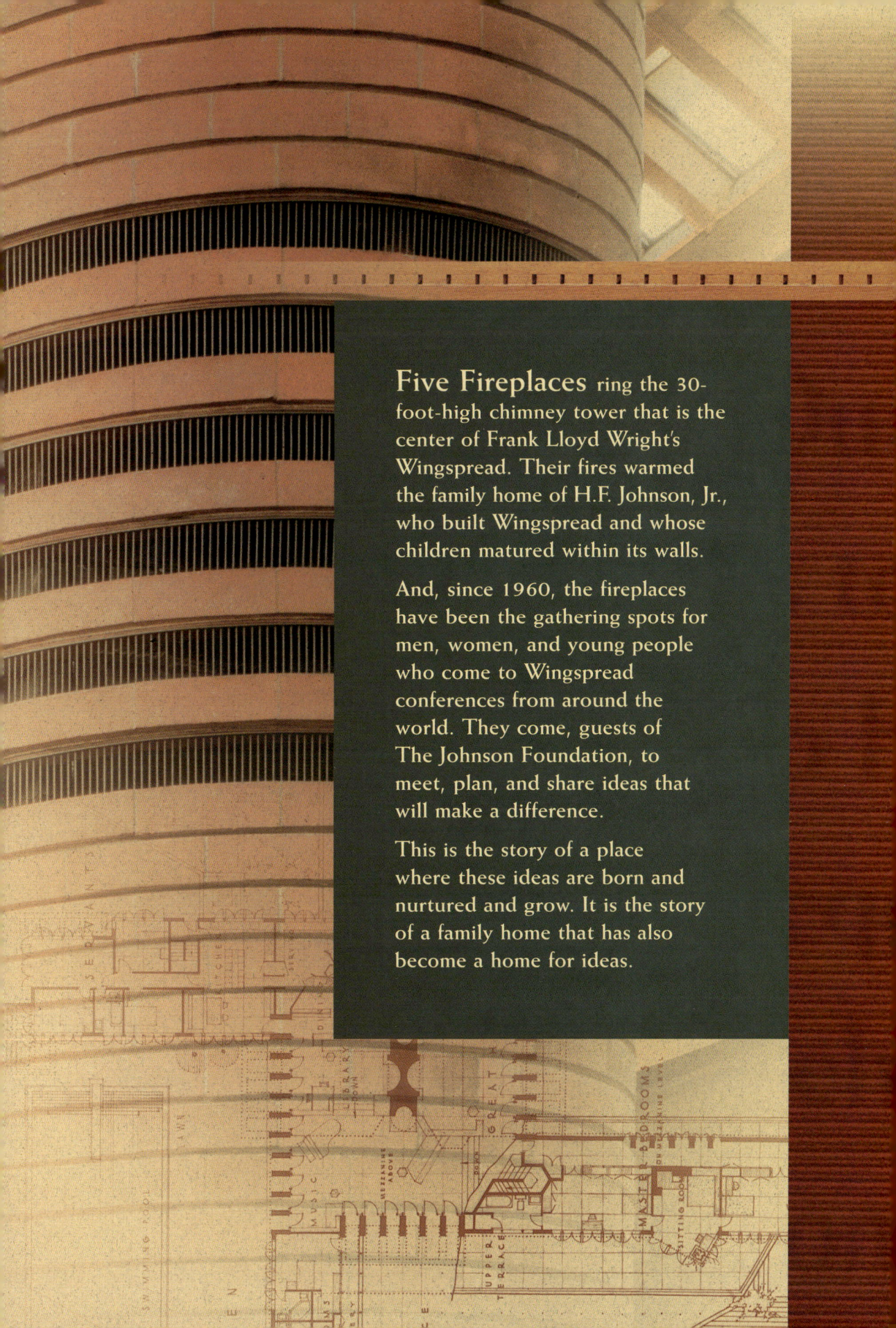

Five Fireplaces ring the 30-foot-high chimney tower that is the center of Frank Lloyd Wright's Wingspread. Their fires warmed the family home of H.F. Johnson, Jr., who built Wingspread and whose children matured within its walls.

And, since 1960, the fireplaces have been the gathering spots for men, women, and young people who come to Wingspread conferences from around the world. They come, guests of The Johnson Foundation, to meet, plan, and share ideas that will make a difference.

This is the story of a place where these ideas are born and nurtured and grow. It is the story of a family home that has also become a home for ideas.

During the 1930s, Herbert F. Johnson (1899-1978) commissioned Frank Lloyd Wright to design a house for him near Racine, Wisconsin. Wright called his creation Wingspread, because its four wings embrace the prairie while the roof over the central Great Hall soars skyward. The Johnsons' later home, "The House," is visible to the right of Wingspread in the aerial photo.

Wingspread is so well-integrated with its natural setting that it wears raiments of snow, wild grapes, and hostas with equal grace. Wright intended Wingspread to be overgrown with native plants, and used architecture to heighten the experience of nature.

Two of Wingspread's most distinctive features—the "crow's nest" aerie towering above the roof, and the long, cantilevered balcony on the north wing—were the ideas of H.F. Johnson's children, Karen and Sam. All the exterior wood is unfinished tidewater cypress, which has weathered to a silvery gray.

The Great Hall shows off Wright's genius as a sculptor of space. Light, shadow, and the interplay of varied materials all contribute to the calm splendor of the combined living, dining, and library areas. Three bands of skylights step up to a 30-foot-high ceiling, and spiral stairs lead up to the crow's nest.

Wright's designs for Wingspread include built-in and freestanding furniture pieces such as couches, ottomans, barrel chairs, and coffee tables. Classic dentils carved in oak appear as a motif throughout the house. Here, *upper left*, a mezzanine-level room as converted for conference use.

The Roots of a Family Enterprise

> **My husband [Frank Lloyd Wright]** always maintained that if he had enough enlightened businessmen for clients he could change the face of the nation, build beautiful buildings for all types of purposes, and thereby make human life more meaningful for the people who live and work in them.
>
> With his client and friend [Herbert] Johnson he found just that sort of person.
>
> — *Olgivanna Wright*

Herbert Fisk Johnson and Frank Lloyd Wright first discussed the house that would become Wingspread in the autumn of 1936. Wright was nearly seventy years old. His reputation as a renowned architect was well established, but the Great Depression had all but extinguished his active career. Between 1928 and 1934, he had designed and built only two houses for clients.

H.F. Johnson was roughly half Wright's age when the two men met. Born in 1899, Johnson was christened Hibbard (often shortened to "Hib"), but later changed his legal name to Herbert. Upon his father's death in 1928, H.F. Johnson assumed leadership of the Johnson Wax Company, which his grandfather had founded in 1886. In spite of his youth and lack of business experience, H.F. Johnson guided the family company to prosperity by the mid-thirties, when the rest of the country was still mired in the Depression. By 1936, Johnson Wax had outgrown its old headquarters in Racine, Wisconsin.

Wright and Johnson, 1937.

Johnson wanted to build a new administration building that would reflect his company's commitment to innovation and a bright future. Rejecting a preliminary plan by a local architect, he hired Wright to design something special.

Wright's design for the Johnson Wax Administration Building was like nothing built before. Architectural critics and historians later hailed it as one of Wright's two or three greatest masterpieces. Johnson already knew he was going to like the new office building when, in the fall of 1936, it was little more than a foundation on a muddy construction site. One day when he and Wright were observing the building's progress, Johnson jokingly told his architect "I think I'll just put a cot in my office and live here."

"Oh, no you won't," Wright replied. "I'll build you a house." Johnson took him at his word. Before long, the house that was to become Wingspread was underway.

The Great Workroom of the Johnson Wax Administration Building was the corporate prelude to Wingspread's Great Hall.

WINGSPREAD'S SITE

> **Should you ever see the house,** observe this fact...the house did something remarkable to that site. The site was not at all stimulating before the house went up—but like developer poured over a negative, when you view the environment framed by the architecture of the house from within, somehow, like magic, charm appears in the landscape and will be there wherever you look. The site seems to come alive.
>
> – Frank Lloyd Wright

For years before he met Wright, Johnson had been buying small adjoining parcels of land in Wind Point, an unincorporated farming community a few miles north of Racine. By 1936, Johnson's holdings in Wind Point consisted of some fifty acres. He dammed a stream that ran through the property to create a pond that could be stocked with fish. A mixture of farmland and woods, the assembled parcel teemed with deer, pheasants, waterfowl, and many other birds. He entertained thoughts of using the Wind Point acreage for hunting and fishing, but eventually dismissed this idea and registered the land as a state wildlife preserve. On weekends, especially in autumn, he took his two children, Karen and Sam, to the property for nature walks and picnics.

Johnson had been a single father until, in 1936 (an eventful year for him), he married Jane Roach, who had two children of her own. The newly expanded family lived in the old Johnson Homestead, a Victorian house built in 1902. Just as the wax company had outgrown its old headquarters, the Johnson family had outgrown the homestead. It was time to build a new house. Johnson's land in Wind Point was the perfect site.

Wingspread's setting as seen from the east in 1939.

A view of the north wing's upper and lower terrace enclosures from the east.

Wingspread's Plan

> **I respect "hunches" of others,** that is, should they correspond with mine! This one—the little sketch made with T-square and triangle—did. Soon that new "zoned" house… was designed, and under way.
>
> — *Frank Lloyd Wright*

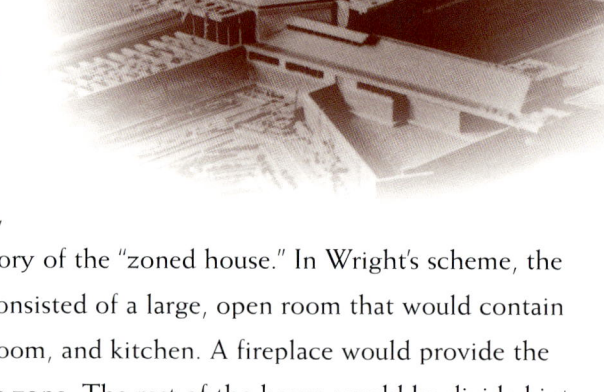

One day in November 1936 Johnson asked Wright to accompany him to his acreage in Wind Point. The two men walked around the property and discussed how a house might be sited on it. During this conversation, Wright described his theory of the "zoned house." In Wright's scheme, the heart of a zoned house consisted of a large, open room that would contain the living room, dining room, and kitchen. A fireplace would provide the focal point for this public zone. The rest of the house would be divided into private zones for various members of the household.

Johnson liked this idea—especially the balance between conviviality and privacy that it offered. He began to elaborate on the concept himself, incorporating features he had seen in other buildings. His strongest source of inspiration, aside from Wright himself, was the Drake Hotel in Chicago. Johnson admired the way the hotel's wings converged in the main lobby, an imposing room with high ceilings and an impressive skylight. Johnson also felt attracted to the freestanding fireplace that dominated the Palm Court, a secondary lobby at the Drake.

Wright inspects a model of Wingspread.

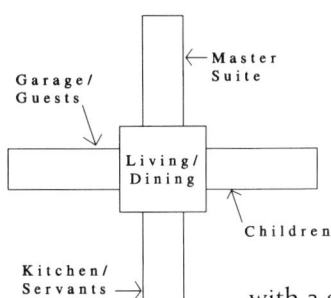

Soon after visiting the Drake Hotel in the winter of 1936–37, Johnson sketched a conceptual floor plan for a new house and presented it to Wright. The plan resembled a big plus-sign with a square superimposed in the middle. The four appendages, or wings, contained zones to which Johnson assigned particular functions. One wing would house the master suite, another would contain children's bedrooms and a playroom, the third would house the kitchen and servants' quarters, and the fourth wing would accommodate guests and a garage. The square in the middle of the sketch represented a big room for living and dining. Johnson suggested to Wright that this central room should have a skylight and a dramatic fireplace in the middle.

Wright did not always respond warmly to sketches drawn by clients. For Johnson's drawing, however, the architect had nothing but praise. Johnson's plan fit exactly with his own ideas of the zoned house. "Hib brought me a little sketch plan he had himself penciled of the general outlines of a house," Wright later wrote. The sketch, he added, was "zoned pretty much as his [house] stands out there now on the prairie."

Wright called Wingspread "the last of the Prairie houses." The reference hearkened back to the years from 1900 to 1911, which historians have called Wright's "Prairie period." Many of the houses Wright designed during this fertile time feature wings radiating from a high, central mass that contains a prominent hearth and chimney. Of these earlier houses, the one that most resembles Wingspread is Wright's 1911 design for Sherman Booth of Glencoe, Illinois.

A floor plan of Wright's unbuilt design for the Sherman Booth house (1911), a Prairie period house that prefigures Wingspread's plan.

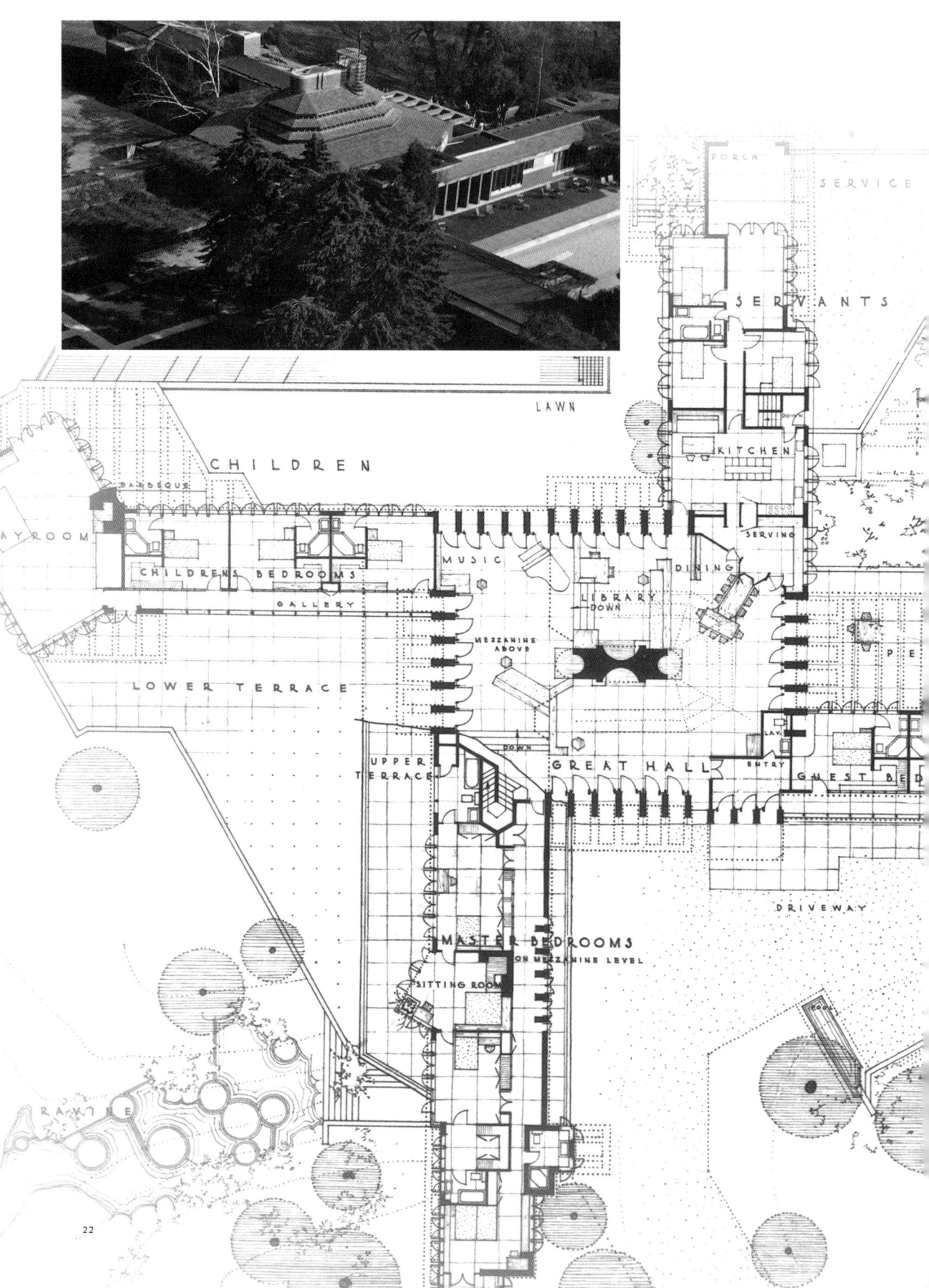

At the center of the four zones the spacious Living Room stands. A tall central chimney-stack with five fireplaces divides this vertical space into spaces for the various domestic functions: Entrance Hall, Family Living Room, Library Living Room, and Dining Room.

Extending from this lofty central room are four wings—three low and one with mezzanine. The one with mezzanine floor and galleries is for the master, mistress, and young daughter. Another wing extends from the central space for their several boys; a playroom at the end, a graduated deep-pool in conjunction; another wing for service and utilities; another for guests and five motor cars.

Each wing has independent views on two sides, each has perfect privacy.

— *Frank Lloyd Wright*

Wright accepted Johnson's zoning assignments for the four wings without change. He modified the placement of the wings, however, so that they connected to the central rectangle at its corners, rather than at the center of each wall. This simple modification transformed the static, cruciform plan into a pinwheel shape, full of implied motion and energy.

An aerial photo taken in 1974.

This blueprint (oriented with the north bedroom wing at the bottom and the south service wing at the top) shows Wingspread's original room layout and the 4-foot by 4-foot grid that Wright used as his basic planning module in this project.

Wingspread and "Organic" Architecture

> **The building as architecture** is born out of the heart of man, permanent consort to the ground, comrade to the trees, true reflection of man in the realm of his own spirit.
>
> — Frank Lloyd Wright

Wright believed strongly in what he called "organic" architecture. An organically designed building, according to his definition, combined the unique characteristics of the site, the climate, the client, and the building process in a single, unified whole. This organic whole would be integrated with nature. He believed that people who inhabited such buildings would become more attuned to their own inner natures.

Wingspread embodies Wright's organic philosophy in many ways. Even more than many of his earlier Prairie houses, Wingspread seems perfectly wedded to its site. Its four wings stretch out to embrace the prairie. Its primary materials—limestone, brick, stucco, and wood—tie the house to the earth, while its many windows and skylights open it to the heavens by admitting air, light, and views of sky and landscape.

After Wright delivered some drawings of the house to Johnson, he wrote a letter to Mrs. Johnson about them. "I hope you will recognize in them a pattern for a happy free life in the country," he wrote. "The plan tangles you up pretty well with sunshine all day long—vistas of outdoors and indoors and privacy for everyone. [It offers] a good basis for domestic happiness."

Wingspread from the northeast shortly after construction was completed.

Wright intended the layered ranks of divided skylights to admit sunlight in patches, creating a dappled effect like that of a forest canopy.

The Construction of Wingspread

> **This is probably one of the most complete,** best constructed...houses it has ever been my good fortune to build.
>
> — *Frank Lloyd Wright*

Work on the house began in April of 1937. Johnson hired Racine builder Ben Wiltscheck for the job. Wiltscheck had a degree in architecture and a good local reputation as a general contractor. Although Wiltscheck had never built any large structures, Johnson had already retained him to oversee construction of the Johnson Wax Administration Building. Wiltscheck had proven himself competent beyond his experience. He was in awe of Wright and adept at executing the architect's designs with faithfulness and patience. He seemed the natural choice for Wingspread.

Wiltscheck hired mostly Scandinavian immigrants to work on his construction crews. The carpenters assigned to Wingspread framed the walls of the north wing—the largest and most complicated of the four—in less than a week. They did such a meticulous job that one of Wright's apprentices compared their rough framing to fine cabinetry work. The masons who later laid up the walls and chimneys proved no less adept.

Wright made a point of combining timeless materials such as brick, stone, and wood, with new products and technologies. Wingspread's heating system, for example, was ahead of its time. It consisted of a boiler, pump, and

Wright likened the Great Hall, when illuminated at night, to a Japanese lantern.

distribution valves that sent hot water through pipes embedded in the concrete floor slab. This system enabled Wright to banish old-fashioned steam radiators so they would not distract from the elegantly simple lines that define each room and space. Unfortunately, however, equipment available in the late 1930s was not up to the job of providing adequate, evenly distributed heat throughout Wingspread's 14,000 square feet of enclosed space. (It was, incidentally, the largest private residence of Wright's design that was ever built.) This early example of radiant-floor heating had to be supplemented with standard forced-air heat in some parts of the house.

After construction had begun, Wright sent notes to Johnson's children, Karen and Sam, asking them to tell him what features they would like to have in their new home. They responded by asking for a lookout tower, reminiscent of the cupola on their maternal grandfather's house. Wingspread's Living Room, with its 30-foot-high ceiling, had already been framed. Adding a lookout tower, therefore, presented some distinct challenges. Wright came up with a fairly simple, elegant solution. The completed crow's nest looked not like an afterthought, but like an essential (albeit whimsical) feature of Wingspread's design.

To emphasize a horizontal linearity, Wright specified that the horizontal grout lines in all of Wingspread's brickwork should be scraped so as to be recessed, while all vertical grout lines should be flush and tinted red so as to resemble the brick.

The north cantilever from the west, top, the pool and southeast terrace.

Equipped with a lockable box for special possessions and a two-way radio, the children's glass-enclosed aerie exceeded Sam and Karen's hopes. From it, they could wave to their father, and even talk to him on the two-way radio when he flew over the house in his private airplane. Karen recalled that climbing up to the crow's nest was like getting into the cockpit of her own airplane, its giant wings (those of the house) majestically spread out below.

Karen also asked Wright if her bedroom could have a long balcony, like one she had seen on his own house at Spring Green. "The girl shall have her balcony," Wright replied. He added a cantilevered balcony to Karen's bedroom at the end of Wingspread's north wing. Of modest length at first, the cantilever grew longer as Wright mused over the drawings. "Every so often at the drawing board," recalled an apprentice, "Mr. Wright would add to it. And add."

The swimming pool, too, was added as an afterthought. Wright welcomed the chance to add what he apparently thought of as a water feature, or reflecting pool, in which swimming was allowed. The pool's side walls are undercut, or recessed a few inches beneath its limestone edge; they also slope outward towards the bottom. "The average swimming pool looks to me like a glorified bath tub," Wright wrote. "There is less sense there of the water than of the basin it is in. With the pool sides undercut you see no walls in the pool but only the water and reflections."

Wingspread was three-fourths complete when, in May 1938, Jane Roach Johnson became gravely ill and passed away. Work on Wingspread ground almost to a halt, and Johnson considered abandoning the project.

Wright, by now Johnson's close friend as well as his architect, urged him to finish the house as a memorial. Johnson finally agreed. "We completed the house in every particular as planned for a wife and four children," Wright concluded, triumphantly. "That house, more than anything else, I believe, brought Hib back again."

Wingspread the Home

> **I have to say that this was a happy place** for my sister and me and our father to live.
>
> — *Samuel C. Johnson*

Sam Johnson was eleven years old when, upon Wingspread's completion in 1939, the family moved into the house. He worried that the change would prove socially disastrous for him, since all his friends lived miles away in southern Racine. He soon discovered, however, that Wingspread's extensive grounds, pond, and swimming pool made the place a boys' paradise. His friends would ride their bicycles up to Wind Point for the day, often spending the night, as well.

Karen enjoyed Wingspread no less than her brother did. "The house just made me feel joyful, and very warm," she said years later. She felt uplifted in the Living Room, in part because it was filled with light in the daytime. At night, the big room with its tall windows and towering bands of skylights glowed like a lantern. On warm days, the family enjoyed eating lunch on one of the terraces. H.F. Johnson said he hated to leave his home in the morning and hated to leave his office in the new Administration Building at the end of the day.

The dining room table with Frank Lloyd Wright barrel chairs made for Wingspread.

Wingspread's complex roof structure leaked from the start. Stories about Wright's roofs are the stuff of architectural legend. Some of these stories are even true—including one about a dinner party that took place at Wingspread. Sam Johnson witnessed it himself. Here's how he once recalled the occasion to a group of architects who had gathered in Wingspread's Living Room:

> *One night my father had some distinguished guests to dinner, and as a thirteen-year-old I was invited to sit at the side of the table and keep quiet. My father had men working very hard for a year with putty guns on the windows in the roof to keep them from leaking. It was successful until a thunderstorm occurred. I looked around a little nervously, and one leak started in the corner where the end of the table was, and the rain came down right on the top of my father's bald head.*
>
> *He went into a rage. There was a phone on a desk in a little alcove near the table, and he asked the maid to give it to him. He sat right where he was as the water leaked down. He picked up the phone and said, "I would like to speak to Mr. Frank Lloyd Wright in Taliesin West in Phoenix, Arizona." Amazingly, in about five minutes, he said, "Frank, you built this beautiful house for me and we enjoy it very much. But I have told you the roof leaks, and right now I am with some friends and distinguished guests and it is leaking right on top of my head." Mr. Wright very clearly came back so that we could all hear it at the table: "Well, Hib, why don't you move your chair?"*

Two years after moving into Wingspread, H.F. Johnson married Irene Purcell, a radio, stage, and screen actress. The couple loved to dance and host parties, and found Wingspread ideal for entertaining. It was, Irene Johnson once said, "the perfect party house." The Johnsons held a Christmas party each year for as many as 150 children of friends and relatives. Their annual New Year's Eve parties featured a live band and much ballroom dancing. At one party, Karen once recalled, she and her friends formed a conga line that snaked from the Living Room to her bedroom and back.

In spite of its virtues as a house for entertaining, Irene Johnson felt somewhat overwhelmed by Wright's architecture. His buildings are notoriously difficult to furnish, because the architecture is so strong that it, in effect, becomes the decor. "It is quite impossible," he once wrote, "to consider the building as one thing and its furnishings another." Much of the furniture in Wingspread is built-in. Wright also designed some freestanding furniture pieces for Wingspread, including a set of 16 barrel chairs, several hexagonal ottomans, and some coffee tables. He selected and hung some Japanese prints in the house before the Johnsons moved in. With that, Wright felt that Wingspread was not only finished, but also fully decorated.

Irene Johnson naturally tried to make her own imprint on the house by hanging some paintings and draperies. She replaced a few chairs and coverings, and even designed some furniture pieces and had them custom-built.

After the Johnsons had been married for a few years, they invited Wright for a visit. He accepted and stayed the night. The next morning, he got up before dawn and redecorated the Living Room. He removed several of Irene Johnson's paintings and furniture pieces, put them in a storeroom, and rehung the original Japanese prints. When the Johnsons came down for breakfast the next morning, Wright was waiting. "Well, how do you like it?" he asked. It was the last night Wright was to spend at Wingspread.

By the mid-1950s, Karen and Sam had grown up and left home. Irene and H.F. Johnson, now "empty nesters," decided to build a smaller house next door. They retained California architect Henry L. Eggers and interior designer T.H. Robsjohn-Gibbings to design a new residence overlooking Wingspread's pond, with its ever-changing populations of migratory birds. The Johnsons called their new home "The House." They moved from Wingspread into The House in 1959.

The Johnsons' subsequent home, The House, as viewed from the east.

Strong geometric lines mark Wingspread inside and out. Above, a view of the Cypress Terrace from the north; below, a portion of the lower living room as seen from the mezzanine.

Wingspread the Conference Center

> **When Frank Lloyd Wright designed** Wingspread, he used, as usual, his prophetic vision. He made Wingspread a social center rather than a home. That is why, today, when Mr. and Mrs. Johnson so graciously are giving up their house in behalf of something greater—the house is absolutely adapted to its new purpose.
>
> — *Olgivanna Wright*

The Johnsons' move necessitated finding a new use for Wingspread. The couple wanted to find an appropriate use for the building while retaining control over the property and ensuring their privacy on the adjoining lot. They chose to donate Wingspread to an existing foundation—The Johnson Foundation, funded mainly by the Johnson Wax Company—that would operate Wingspread as a center for educational conferences. In 1959, the existing charitable trust was reorganized as The Johnson Foundation, Inc., an independent operating foundation that would be supported by income from endowments and by contributions from the company and the Johnson family.

In order to serve its new function as a conference center, Wingspread required a general reassignment of room functions along with some physical modifications. The large playroom in the east wing (now called the Terrace Room) became a good space for conference plenary sessions. The three

A plaque commemorating the dedication of Wingspread for use as a conference center.

adjacent bedrooms became a theater conference room, a conference office, and a recording room. Similarly, the bedrooms on the mezzanine level in the north wing were converted into meeting rooms, while the area beneath them provided space for public restrooms and a cloak room. The servants' quarters in the south wing made ideal offices for Johnson Foundation staff. When more staff office space was needed, the bays of the carport in the west wing were enclosed in a manner that is all but indistinguishable from Wingspread's original architecture.

The central core of the house would now serve three purposes: as a public living room, as a dining room for as many as seventy people, and as a conference, auditorium, or performance space that could seat as many as 100. Additional wiring for more lights, televisions, and telephones was installed, as was an improved ventilation and air-conditioning system.

Wright had designed an emblem for Wingspread when the house was completed. It consisted, basically, of a decorated circle with stylized wings projecting from it. Inscribed in the circle were Johnsons' initials, H.F.J., JR. In 1961, one of Wright's former apprentices redesigned the Wingspread logo

Wright designed this original bronze casting, inscribed with H.F. Johnson, Jr.'s, initials and set in concrete at Wingspread's main entrance.

*A view of the living room, top.
Olgivanna Wright and H.F. Johnson lead a procession on the day of
Wingspread's dedication to The Johnson Foundation, June 24, 1961.*

so it could serve as an emblem for The Johnson Foundation, now headquartered there. In the new emblem, Wright's original design was simplified, its style subtly updated. In the center of the new design are the initials "TJF."

H.F. and Irene Johnson formally dedicated Wingspread to The Johnson Foundation at a ceremony held on June 24, 1961. More than 100 people attended, including Johnson Wax Company executives, prominent Racinians, Johnson family members, the Foundation's board of trustees, and its new president, Leslie Paffrath. In dedicating the building, H.F. Johnson said that he expected the Foundation to promote educational excellence, international understanding, intellectual and cultural growth, and "our own overseas 'people-to-people' program."

Wright died in 1959 while Wingspread's conversion to a conference center was just getting underway. His widow, Olgivanna, attended the dedication ceremony and gave a brief speech. "When I came to Wingspread this morning," she said, "I felt real conviction that this now will be a perfect place for enlightened dialogues, discussions, conferences, and lectures. I know that if Mr. Wright were standing here instead of me, he would say the same thing."

In closing, she said, "Whoever will come to Wingspread will find the sight of this beautiful building an edifying experience in itself." Olgivanna's prediction has proven true with each of the thousands of conferences and events The Johnson Foundation has held at Wingspread. As a veteran of several Wingspread conferences recently put it,

> *When you go into Wingspread, the experience has the capacity to transform. Part of it is the warm tones, the wood, the fireplaces. Even in summer, when the fireplaces are idle, the hearths project a warm, tranquil quality. The atmosphere invites reflection, but not passive reflection.*
>
> *The unusual design of the house is an ever-present reminder that new thought is possible.*

Ready to Serve in a New Century

> We called the house "Wingspread" because spread its wings it would... wings in more than one sense.
>
> — *Frank Lloyd Wright*

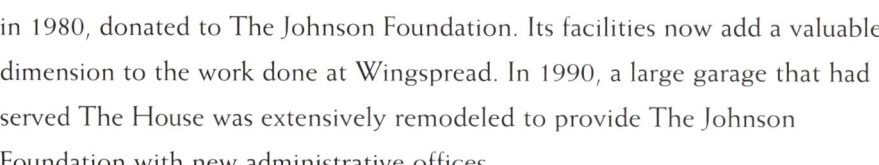

H.F. Johnson died in December 1978. The House was then remodeled for conference use and, in 1980, donated to The Johnson Foundation. Its facilities now add a valuable dimension to the work done at Wingspread. In 1990, a large garage that had served The House was extensively remodeled to provide The Johnson Foundation with new administrative offices.

The U.S. Secretary of the Interior designated Wingspread as a National Historic Landmark in 1990. Since then, Wingspread the building has undergone a series of repairs, all of them subject to the stringent preservation requirements to which all National Historic Landmarks are subject.

Much of the work has been focused on repairing and restoring Wingspread's one-of-a-kind roof. The most extensive round of repairs, which took place from 1994–97, required that Wingspread be closed to the public. Scaffolding filled the Living Room, temporarily supporting its multi-tiered roof while workers surgically replaced rafters from above. Then the whole roof was stabilized with layers of a composite-fiber diaphragm, a material that is normally used in building high-performance yacht hulls.

With the reopening of Wingspread in the summer of 1997, The Johnson Foundation fixed its compass on a more sharply defined direction: the idea of sustainable community.

Conceived and built during the first half of the 20th century, Wingspread stands at the beginning of the 21st century as a reinvigorated symbol of new thought and innovation.

Wingspread was named a National Historic Landmark in 1990. Though many alterations and repairs have been made since the building's completion in 1939, all changes have been made with Wright's vision and intent foremost in mind.

Wright designed forms intended to evoke the ancient elements of earth, air, fire, and water. The living room glows at night like a fire-filled lantern. Built on a limestone base, the low, horizontal house reflects the earth's striated layers. The pool and the soaring skylights exemplify Wright's evocation of water and air.

42

Wright used materials as a painter uses texture and color. In Wingspread, his palette included tinted stucco, red Streator bricks, slabs of Kasota limestone, red-clay roofing tiles, unstained cypress siding, white oak for interior woodwork, and tinted concrete for floors. The house was designed on a 4-foot by 4-foot grid; most of the doors and windows are positioned in conformity with this pattern.

H.F. Johnson loved fireplaces.

Wingspread contains eight—five in the massive central hearth, one in the children's playroom (now called the Terrace Room), one in the sitting room *below*, and one outdoors on the terrace by the swimming pool. For Johnson, the hearth carried connotations of both conviviality and privacy, a duality that Wingspread was designed not just to accommodate, but to honor.

Acknowledgements

Cover photo by Thomas A. Heinz

Photo credits:

Gerald Cross/Imagehaus: pages 9, 10

Samuel H. Gottscho, the Gottscho Collection, courtesy of the Library of Congress: pages 8, 13, 18, 24, 26, 27, 33, 39, 40

Ray Hartl: pages 11, 13, 33, 39, 42, 43

Thomas A. Heinz: pages 6, 7, 8, 9, 11, 13, 14, 15, 25, 28, 30, 32, 36, 38, 40, 41, 42, 44, 45, 46, 47

The Johnson Foundation archives: pages 10, 19, 20, 28, 34, 35, 36, 43

SC Johnson & Son, Inc.: pages 16, 17, 22

Frank Lloyd Wright drawings are copyright © The Frank Lloyd Wright Foundation, Scottsdale, Arizona: pages 21, 22, cover

Sources:

Information and ideas drawn in part from a Wingspread display and other material by Jonathan Lipman and Cooper Norman of Prairie Architects.

Design & Production:

Design by Hare Strigenz, Inc., Milwaukee, Wisconsin

Printed by CastlePierce, Oshkosh, Wisconsin

Printed on Ikono Dull Satin, a 50% recycled paper by Zanders with 20% post-consumer waste fiber, processed totally chlorine free. Printed with soy ink and aqueous coating.

Published by The Johnson Foundation, Inc., P.O. Box 547, Racine, Wisconsin 53401-0547. Copyright © The Johnson Foundation, Inc., 1997.

Printed in the United States of America